Whiskey & Wisdom

A watercolor journey through Irish sayings and proverbs.

France Austin Miller & Yvonne Foster

RED SABLE
PRESS

P.O. Box 345
Bayfield, Wisconsin

Published in the United States of America by:
Red Sable Press
P.O. Box 345
Bayfield, WI 54814

Printed in the United States of America by:
The Imaging Bureau
4545 Cambridge Rd.
Fort Worth, TX 76155

First Printing, First Edition
Marketed by Red Sable Press

ISBN 978-0-9785635-0-9
ISBN 0-9785635-0-6

What fills the eye, fills the heart.

Spiral in the trees near Ross Castle, County Kerry, Ireland.

Painting with a group is a magical experience. When the room grows quiet, the magic begins.

I've been conducting watercolor workshops for 15 years, and I remember each one of them, by the pithy comments that waft through the room (usually anonymous because it is hard to look up when you're painting), and through the emerging paintings that pop out for critique like spring crocuses. I recall past students not in conjunction with a name, but with an image. I remember their struggles and joys and the sighs, whispers and snarls.

The magic begins when we plan a workshop (a year in advance), often making dear friends in foreign countries well before leaving home. This magic weaves through the group pulling us gently together until the unity of the painting experience begins to present itself as an entity. Our workshop in Ireland proved magical from the moment we glimpsed the kaleidoscope of lush Irish greens through the gray morning mist on our low approach into the Shannon Airport.

The Newgrange symbol (a spiral like image), is easily found in Joey Kartarik's photo, on the facing page, from Ireland's Killarney National Park. Joey spotted the spiral in the trees and snapped the picture, unaware that Ruth Yokum was concurrently taking a similar photograph three miles down the path. The Newgrange spiral is one of the country's oldest stone carvings (3200 B.C.), and is prominently woven throughout the Irish culture. It became our workshop's talisman, a faithful reappearing presence, forming a binding connection to the essence of Ireland.

Upon returning from the Ireland 2005 workshop, I wrote the following to my co-editor, Yvonne Foster, about the making of this book:

"I want the reader to get the essence, an experience, a feeling for the magic of the country itself. We use our spiral (Newgrange) photos, we let it be known that Ireland took us on a journey of its own.

"Irish sayings, toasts and blessings offer humor, beauty and truth, the trinity of success for vision. These three spiritual entities seem to come along with us on our jaunts like angels in the back seat, and I think we can get them into a book.

"This is what I envision, not an Irish travel journal, or just some cute watercolors about fools born every minute and front door knockers. The greatness of our group of painters lies in the pure good-hearted emotions that cascade into their paintings, and couple beautifully with Irish wisdom."

I am truly grateful to co-editor, Yvonne Foster, and our workshop planner and guide, Michele Auger Eldred. Friends forever. And to the patient, good-natured and loyal painters who travel with us, there is not a clunker in the bunch.

France Austin Miller

whiskey & wisdom

Wisdom...

      everyone is wise until he speaks.

There's a fool born every minute
and every one of them lives.

Whoever the cap fits, take it.

whiskey & wisdom

You'll never plow a field
by turning it over in your mind.

YM Foster

It's no secret if it's known to three.

whiskey & wisdom

It destroys the craft not to learn it.

May the hinges of our friendship never grow rusty.

About evening a man is known.

whiskey & wisdom

No forcing the sea.

whiskey & wisdom

Slainte!

Drink is the curse of the land.
It makes you fight with your neighbor.
It makes you shoot at your landlord.
And it makes you miss him.

Good as drink is,
it ends in thirst.

What whiskey and butter won't cure,
there is no cure for.

Here's to lying, stealing and cheating.
May you lie to save a friend,
may you steal the heart of the one you love,
and may you cheat death.

Women do not drink liquor but
it disappears when they are present.

May those that love us, love us.
And those that don't love us.
may God turn their hearts.

And if He doesn't turn their hearts,
may He turn their ankles,
so we'll know them by their limping.

Time is a good storyteller.

A proverb cannot be bettered.

God is good—but never dance in a small boat.

The road to heaven is well sign-posted
but not well lit.

It's no use carrying an umbrella,
if your shoes are leaking.

Jayne Findler

Marriages are all happy—
it's having breakfast together that causes
all the trouble.

We hold our children's hands but a short while,
and their hearts forever.

There's many a good tune played on an old fiddle.

There's no hearth
like your own hearth.

May your homes always be too small
to house all of your friends.

Castles were built one stone at a time.

Even a tin knocker shines on a dirty door.

The smaller the cabin, the wider the door.

The doorstep to a great house is slippery.

Ann Lacey

May the roof above us never fall in.
And may the friends gathered below it
never fall out.

The eye should be blind in the home of another.

whiskey & wisdom

There is no strength without unity.

THE ARTISTS

1. **France Austin Miller.** France and her family make their home in Lake Superior's north woods, where, in 1984 they established the Austin Miller Studio, near Bayfield, Wisconsin. Quote the artist: "I am bound by the love and humor of family & friends and the beauty of Lake Superior, life is good." www.austinmillerstudio.com

2. **Ann Locey.** Ann is an interior designer by profession and has been totally enlightened by being in France Austin Miller's study trips for the past three years and painting watercolors for the first time. Using ink for definition with strong, intense colors on hot press paper has defined her unique style.

3. **Annie Harris.** Annie is a summer resident on Madeline Island and winters in Florida. She has A.F.A. from Bennett College, B.F.A. from University of Arizona, and graduate classes from University of Minnesota. She has had shows throughout the United States, with her paintings being held in corporate and public collections. www.annieharris.com

4. **Yvonne Foster.** Yvonne is journaling this stage of her life in her paintings--watercolors, oils and acrylics. She makes paper and artist's books too, but feels her family is her greatest creation. Home is Madeline Island, Wisconsin, and Minneapolis, Minnesota, with frequent detours to Ireland with her Irish-born husband.

5. **Michele Auger Eldred.** Michele lives on Madeline Island in Lake Superior with her husband and two sons. Being drawn to the creative process her whole life, she is a professional weaver and tour guide by trade. She finds working with watercolor one of the biggest challenges and rewards in her life.

1. France Austin Miller 2. Ann Locey 3. Annie Harris 4. Yvonne Foster 5. Michele Auger Eldred 6. Kelly Kirchner Nelson 7. Jayne Findlen 8. Joey Kartarik 9. Lavetta Torke 10. Ruth Yokum.

6. Kelly Kirchner Nelson. Kelly is fueled by the energy of juxtaposing colors, creating in the moment, cowboy boots, her son's spirit, and the next serendipitous adventure; rejuvenated from family time, searching for beach glass, the camaraderie of women and experiencing life's journey; passionate for pearls, full moons, worn denim, fresh flowers and Madeline Island.

7. Jayne Findlen. Jayne began watercolor painting on Madeline Island, Wisconsin, her summer residence, in 1997. Painting has introduced her to many wonderful places and friends. In real life, she lives with her husband and two beautiful daughters, enjoying life on the ocean in Dorado, Puerto Rico.

8. Joey Kartarik. Joey picked up a paintbrush as a way to express her thoughts about the world. She paints not only what is seen, but what she imagines something to be. Mostly it is a joyous and wonderful experience. Home is with her family on a small lake in Minnesota.

9. Lavetta Torke. Lavetta, a wife, mother and grandmother, retired seven years ago and shares her love of gardening, golf, cooking and art with family and friends. Bayfield is home when she and her husband Tom are not traveling, which stimulates their artistic temperaments and keeps them in contact with their seven children.

10. Ruth Yokum. Ruth, brand new to the exciting world of watercolor, is at home in Lake Elmo, Minnesota, and Florida. Life revolves around family and travel, and she is really enjoying it.

INDEX

All happy endings
are beginnings as well.

To Order more copies of **Whiskey & Wisdom**

By telephone: Call 715-779-5336
By email: franci@centurytel.net
By mail: Use the following form:

ORDER FORM
(This page may be reproduced.)

_____ copies of **Whiskey & Wisdom** @ $14.95/each _____
($17.95 CAN)

Wisconsin orders add 5.5% sales tax . . . _____

Shipping and Handling . . . . _____
$4.00 for 1st book, $2.00 each additional
book; International shipping $9.00 for
1st book, $5.00 each additional book

TOTAL AMOUNT ENCLOSED _____

Make checks or money orders payable to: Red Sable Press

Send order to: Red Sable Press
PO Box 345
Bayfield WI 54814 USA

Credit Card: ❑ Visa   ❑ MasterCard

Card Number _____

Name on card _____ Exp. date _____

Ship To:

Name _____

Address _____

City _____ State _____ Zip _____

Telephone _____